POCKET IMAGES

Bromley, Keston & Hayes

The High Street, 1856. This very early photograph was taken outside the Rising Sun. George Parker, the landlord, had come from Lincoln. The pub was the headquarters of the Society of Bromley Youths, the local bellringers. Next to the pub there was a blacksmith's forge in operation until 1919.

POCKET IMAGES

Bromley, Keston & Hayes

Mick Scott

NONSUCH

First published 1993
This new pocket edition 2007
Images unchanged from first edition

Nonsuch Publishing
Cirencester Road, Chalford
Stroud, Gloucestershire, GL6 8PE
www.nonsuch-publishing.com

Nonsuch Publishing is an imprint of NPI Media Group

British Library Cataloguing in Publication Data.
A catalogue record for this book is available from the British Library.

ISBN 978-1-84588-408-6

Typesetting and origination by NPI Media Group
Printed in Great Britain

Contents

Dunn's, Market Square, Bromley, c. 1930. When these premises were rebuilt a stone inscribed JD 1710 was found, so the family may have been in business here for over 250 years. The shop finally closed in 1980.

Introduction

The London Borough of Bromley is the largest of the London Boroughs, covering an area of over sixty square miles. It stretches from the Crystal Palace in the north to Pratts Bottom in the south and includes the towns and villages of Beckenham, Penge, Anerley, West Wickham, Chislehurst, Petts Wood, Mottingham, Hayes, Keston, Biggin Hill, the Crays, Downe, Cudham, Chelsfield, Farnborough and Green Street Green. Today the population numbers 293,000 and the area is a thriving and popular London suburb. In the north and west it is urbanized, while in the south-east there are acres of rich farmland and wooded hills.

This collection of photographs covers the area that was the old Borough of Bromley, that is Bromley, Hayes and Keston. Bromley was incorporated as a Borough in 1903 and was joined by Hayes and Keston in 1934.

The history of Bromley is closely connected with the See of Rochester. In AD 862 Ethelbert, the King of Kent, made a grant of land to form the Manor of Bromley. It came into the possession of the bishops of Rochester in the tenth century and was held by them until 1845. Soon after the Norman Conquest one of the bishops built a palace which was subsequently rebuilt in 1775, this building now forming the nucleus of the civic offices. In the grounds of the Palace is a chalybeate spring which was dedicated to St Blaise and brought pilgrims to Bromley in the past to drink the waters.

The other building in the town to have a connection with the See is Bromley College. The College, an almshouse, is the oldest building of its kind in England and still continues its original work. The founder, John Warner, Bishop of Rochester, died in 1666 and left £8,500 in his will to build a college for twenty poor widows of clergymen. The original building, a quadrangle with cloisters, remains almost unchanged. A second quadrangle was added in the early nineteenth century and further homes were added in 1840 for the widows' daughters, who could only live in the college while their mothers were alive.

The parish church of St Peter and St Paul dates back to the thirteenth century but only the fourteenth-century tower survived the blitz in 1941 which damaged or destroyed eight Bromley churches.

The bishops, as Lords of the Manor, were granted a charter to hold a market in 1205, and a second, granted by King Henry VI in 1447, allowed a fair which was held twice a year in February and July. A weekly market was held in the town square and by the end of the eighteenth century Bromley was an important centre of a thriving rural community. Sited on the main road from London to Sevenoaks, Tunbridge Wells and the south, the town became a busy coach stop, and inns like the White Hart and the Bell supplied this lucrative trade.

The bishops left the Palace in 1845 and many local residents felt that Bromley's position as a leading town in the county was threatened. However, in 1858 the first railway line was opened through the town and the new railway station at Shortlands linked Bromley with London. Many people wishing to work in the metropolis while living in the country found Bromley an ideal spot, and the rapid growth of the town can be dated from this time. Large estates such as that at Bickley were developed and housing spilled over Bromley Common.

A Local Board was first elected in 1867, to be superseded by an Urban District Council in 1894. These bodies, and in 1903 the new Borough, provided the civic amenities required for a growing town, including schools, libraries and a water supply. Today Bromley is an important commercial centre and many people visit the town for business, shopping and pleasure.

The name Hayes means 'village on the heath'. Man has been active in this area back to the time of the Romans and it would seem likely that there was a church here in 1177, as there is a document of that date bearing the name Hayes. A tax roll of 1301 gives the names of twenty-six families living in the village, but a plague in 1349 halved the population. William Pitt the elder bought the Hayes Place estate, and his second son William was born here and baptized in the parish church of St Mary the Virgin. Many famous men visited Hayes Place and both Nelson and Wellington are said to have planted trees in the grounds. Although Pitt sold the estate and moved to Somerset, he purchased it again in 1766 and lived there until his death in 1778. Sir Everard Hambro later lived at the estate and on his death it was sold, the house demolished, and in the 1930s housing was built on the land.

Keston is rich in archaeological evidence, including flint implements from the Stone Age, Iron Age earthworks and a Roman cemetery. The area is referred to in the Domesday Book of 1086 as Chestan. The first large estate in the area was Holwood, which dates back to 1484. In 1785 this estate was purchased by William Pitt the younger, who had some of the earthworks levelled to improve the view! It was under an oak tree in his grounds that his friend William Wilberforce resolved to work to abolish the slave trade. The present Holwood House was designed by Decimus Burton in 1827. Still to be seen in the area is the oldest windmill in Kent, dated 1716, and the source of the River Ravensbourne.

These photographs have been chosen from Bromley's extensive Local Studies collection, and for every photograph that was chosen many more had to be rejected. The rest of the collection, as well as the large library of books, newspapers, maps and ephemera, and the archive collection may be seen at the Central Library in Bromley High Street.

Mick Scott
Senior Librarian, Local Studies
London Borough of Bromley

One

Bromley

The Old Market House from the south-east, c. 1860. It is thought that this was built between 1729 and 1732, when a record of it first appeared in the Poor Rate Book. It had a red-tiled roof surmounted by a small cupola with a fleur-de-lis finial. Projecting at first-floor level was a sloping roof supported by oak posts and trusses, under which tradesmen were allowed to shelter their carts. On the first floor of the Market House was a room that seated 200 people. Lectures and public entertainments were held here.

Opposite above: The Market House fell into disrepair and was known locally as the 'old shed'. It was finally demolished in 1863. The town pump can be seen in the foreground.

Opposite below: The events held in Market Square included weekly markets, fairs and local elections. The Bromley Fair dates back to a charter of 1447, which was granted by King Henry VI to the bishop of Rochester, lord of the manor. The fair was held twice a year on the feasts of St James, 25 July and St Blaise< 3 February. The Rose and Crown is on the left of the picture.

Market Square, c. 1900.

Market Square and the Town Hall, c. 1900. Until it was moved into the new Town Hall, the police station for the area was in the building occupied later by the Forester Inn.

12

The High Street and Market Square, c. 1905. This postcard view shows the drinking fountain

The Market, c. 1909. The centre of Bromley hosted the market until the needs of local traffic forced the stalls off the streets. The atmosphere in the market-place was not always pleasant, the Bromley Record for 1883 including the following poem, which complained about the activities of a tallow melting and soap boiling works:

'Oh! smells of grease, Oh! smells of grease,
Pervading Market Square,
Oh, will you never, never cease
To poison Bromley's air?'

A busy day in Market Square.

Market Square in the 1920s.

The High Street, Bromley, c. 1898. The Star and Garter was built in the late eighteenth century. Nalder and Collyer was a Croydon brewery.

Opposite above: Aberdeen Buildings were begun in 1887 by Amos Bore and were completed during 1889. The buildings have been restored and are still in use today.

Opposite below: Nos 40–3 High Street, c. 1882.

The corner of Beckenham Lane and the High Street, c. 1905.

The High Street, looking towards the Market Place, 1905. The Royal Bell is on the left.

Looking north along the High Street towards London Road. The Bell Hotel is advertising posthorses.

High Street, c. 1905. The area on the left was known as the New Road or the New Cut, and by 1905 was almost totally occupied by Medhurst's Stores. No. 47 was the china, glass and pottery emporium of Joseph Wells. On 21 September 1866 his son Herbert George was born there. H.G. Wells spent much of his childhood in the town, until at the age of 13 he was apprenticed to a draper and left the area.

High Street, looking towards Beckenham Lane corner.

The Broadway, an impressive row of shops along one side of the road, was begun by 1885 and completed by 1906-7. Sloping down towards the station, it provided premises for tradesmen eager to attract the custom of those arriving in the town by train.

The Broadway and Bromley South station.

The High Street and the public library, which was opened in 1906.

The High Street before the road widening scheme, November 1935.

High Street, looking down towards Mason's Hill, November 1935. The Railway Signal was opened to cater for the railway trade, and closed in 1987.

The High Street, looking north towards the library in the 1930s. The Methodist church on the right opened in 1875.

The High Street, looking south, November 1935.

The Broadway, c. 1938.

Looking north along the High Street, c. 1958. Wilson's Café was a noted local landmark, and the smell of roasting coffee was a familiar one to many shoppers.

High Street, c. 1958.

High Street, c. 1958. A view from the top of Church Road, looking north.

Swan Hill, c. 1900.

East Street, c. 1871–2. East and West Streets were built along the edge of a triangular field called the Cage Field. The Cage itself was a small nineteenth-century prison consisting of two cells. In this photograph can be seen the Drill Hall and Local Board offices.

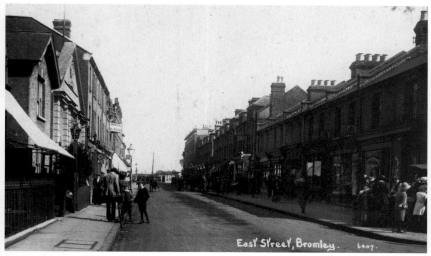

East Street, c. 1912.

London Road junction with Tweedy Road, c. 1920. Looking north, Tweedy Road is on the right. Joseph Follett and Sons were local bakers.

Church Road, looking east towards the Market Square. The rear of Church House Lodge is on the right.

Church House Lodge, Church Road. This Victorian lodge is still to be seen today.

The River Ravensbourne at Queen's Mead. Two postmen are on their rounds.

Above: Martin's Hill and Queen's Mead from Glassmill Lane. Martin's Hill was purchased by the Local Board in 1878 and the meadows and hop gardens were acquired in 1887. The latter were bought and renamed Queen's Mead to honour the Jubilee of Queen Victoria. The River Ravensbourne provided the power for a mill in this area from the time of the Domesday Book, 1086. In the nineteenth century this mill was used to grind mirrors and lenses, hence Glassmill Lane.

Opposite below: Bromley Hill Lodge, Beckenham Lane. This lodge to the Bromley Hill estate was designed by Lady Farnborough and built by her husband in 1825. The cattle trough was fed by a local spring.

Right: Bromley Hill Lodge, c. 1902. There were three lodges to the Bromley Hill estate. This lodge at the corner of Highland Road provided a carriage exit on to Beckenham Lane.

Below: Beckenham Lane, Shortlands. The railway station to serve Bromley opened at Shortlands in May 1858. People arriving by train still had an uphill walk to the town centre. Local tradesmen took advantage of this passing trade and developed what became Shortlands village. The land had been pasture, with a marshy area to the north of the river known as Frog Island.

Beckenham Lane, Shortlands, looking north from the junction of Beckenham Lane and Meadow Road. Shortlands post office is on the corner.

Beckenham Lane, Shortlands.

34

Widmore Road, c. 1860. In 1815 there was a small hamlet one mile to the east of Bromley called Widmore, or sometimes Wigmore. Widmore Road connected the hamlet to the town centre. On the left can be seen the Cage, a small prison of two cells where drunks and petty criminals were kept overnight. The building next to it was the parish engine house where the fire engine was kept.

Widmore Road, c. 1905. Looking east from the Market Square, the Congregational church can be seen on the right.

The junction of Park Road and Widmore Road. The building in the centre is the Phillips Memorial Hospital. This homoeopathic hospital was opened in 1889 as a memorial to Dr Robert Phillips, a well-respected MD who lived at Burlington House, 118 Widmore Road.

Park Road and Widmore Road, c. 1905.

Widmore Road, c. 1931.

Widmore Green, looking towards the Parade at the corner of Widmore Road and Plaistow Lane, c. 1909.

This is the gateway to the Elizabethan house known as the Old Cottage, Widmore. It bears the date 1599. The inn sign for the Bird in Hand is on the right.

Cottages, Chislehurst Road, Bickley.

Bickley Point, at the junction of Bickley Road, Bickley Park Road, Southborough Road and Page Heath Lane, c. 1908. Bickley cricket ground is behind the house on the left.

CHISLEHURST ROAD. BICKLEY KENT

Well Cottage, Chislehurst Road, Bickley.

Simpsons Road, c. 1915. Simpsons Road takes its name from a fortified and moated house nearby called Simpson's Place, which by the early nineteenth century was in ruins. It is said that the area is haunted by the ghost of a white lady carrying a lighted torch. Bromley South station can be seen in the background.

Opposite above: Plaistow Green, the junction of Burnt Ash Lane, Plaistow Lane and College Road, c. 1895. The wall surrounded Plaistow Hall, an early eighteenth-century house, which was demolished in 1900.

Opposite below: Westmoreland Road was formerly called South Hill Park, and in 1880 boasted six houses.

Mason's Hill, looking towards the railway bridge and Bromley South station, c. 1880. Before the construction of the railway this area was noted for its gravel pits, which provided material for road making.

Opposite above: Mason's Hill, looking south from the railway bridge towards Mason's Hill School, c. 1880. The school opened in 1871 close to the site of the pound, where stray animals were kept until collected by their owners.

Opposite below: Mason's Hill, looking south. Mason's Hill was widened in 1906 at a cost of £922. A local landowner Mr Eley Soames gave a strip of his land to aid the project. Mr Soames also donated part of the site for St Mark's church. The entrance to the Bromley Cottage Hospital is on the right.

4373   MASONS HILL.   BROMLEY.

Oakley Road, Bromley Common. The area from Mason's Hill to Keston Mark was known as Bromley Common. This land was owned by the bishops of Rochester as lords of the manor but they granted 'commoners' rights' to the local inhabitants. This area was enclosed completely under an Act of Parliament of 1821, and from that time development of Bromley Common as a new town began. Oakley Road, running from the main road to Keston Mark, takes its name from Oakley House. The public house in the background is the Two Doves.

Bromley Common, looking north-west between the junctions of Crown Lane and Johnson Road, c. 1910.

Two

Houses

Bromley Palace is one of the most imposing buildings in the Borough. The estate came into the possession of the See of Rochester in the early tenth century. The bishops remained as lords of the manor until 1845. A Palace was built here soon after the Norman Conquest, and was rebuilt in 1775.

The Palace and the large estates that surrounded it were sold to Mr Coles Child, a wealthy coal merchant, in 1845. He extended the house and improved the estates. In 1933 Stockwell College, a teacher training college, moved into the building, and today it forms the nucleus of the council offices for the London Borough of Bromley.

Bromley Palace, 1870.

Opposite above: Bromley Palace lodge and gate, c. 1900.

Opposite below: St Blaise's Well is to be found in the grounds of the Palace. This chalybeate well was thought to have healing properties and was popular with pilgrims. It is dedicated to St Blaise, the Bishop of Sebaste in Armenia, who was martyred in AD 316. He was the patron saint of woolcombers, and therefore a favourite saint of the local Kent wool trade. An annual fair was held on his Saint's day in February in the Market Square.

Neelgherries was a large house on the site of the present library and theatre complex. George Sparkes, a civil servant, retired from India in 1848 and purchased his old school, renaming it Neelgherries. He eventually married his housekeeper Emily and educated her. On her death at the age of 90 in 1900 she left the house and grounds to the Town for 'an institution or establishment for the public benefit', and in 1906 a new public library was opened on the site (see p. 106).

Opposite above: Church House, c. 1920. This was built on the site of an earlier house in 1832 by the Bishop's trustees. The grounds, lawns and fishponds were added by Abel Moysey in the late 1830s. The house was purchased by the Town Council in 1926 and during the war, until it was bombed in 1941, was used by the Royal Observer Corps.

Opposite below: Elmfield is an attractive house at Bromley Common, and dates from the eighteenth century. This listed building has been used as a school and a nursing home.

Blackbrook, Southborough. The estate can be traced back to the thirteenth century. The house was the home of George Eliot, the novelist, for a few months in 1873. It was destroyed by fire in February 1897.

Freelands, Plaistow Lane, was converted into a convent in 1888.

Above: The Rookery, Bromley Common, before the alterations of 1890. During the war this property was used as a Biggin Hill operations room during part of the Battle of Britain. It was damaged by fire while occupied by the RAF. Bromley College of Technology now occupies this site.

Sundridge Park. The Sundridge Park estate can be dated back to the Conquest, the first owners, the de Blound family, coming over with William the Conqueror from Normandy. In 1793 the then owner, Mr Edward George Lind, commissioned the noted landscape gardener Humphrey Repton to report on the estate. Repton wrote that the house should be demolished as he considered it to be in the wrong place. Lind, on the strength of this report, sold the estate for £6,000, making a loss of £10,000. The new owner, Mr Claude Scott of Chislehurst, accepted the report and the present house was built.

Opposite below: Bromley Hill is a large house on the London Road. Part of its estate is today in the London Borough of Lewisham. From 1801 to 1838 the house was the home of Lord and Lady Farnborough. They entertained George IV, William IV and Queen Adelaide here, and William Pitt was a frequent guest. During the First World War the house served as a hospital, and today it is a hotel.

Sundridge Park was designed by an associate of Repton, the noted architect John Nash. The mansion is a fine example of the architecture of the period, with beautiful plasterwork and staircases. A noted golf club was formed here in 1901, and in 1920 the house became a country hotel. Today it is a management training centre.

Three

Businesses and Trade

Above: The White Hart Inn can be dated to 1509 by a will of Robert Beckyngham. It is quite possible, though, that the inn dated back to the fourteenth century, as the sign showed the badge of Richard II (1377–99). In the 1830s the landlord William Pawley extended the building to make it a large coaching inn for the town. He also added a spacious assembly room, where balls, political and parochial meetings, concerts and lectures were held until the opening of the Town Hall in 1863. The 18th Kent Rifle Volunteers were formed here in 1859, and until the fire station in West Street was opened in 1868 the Volunteer Fire Brigade had their headquarters here.

The rear of the Royal Bell Hotel. Opposite the Royal Bell were the premises of the famous surgeon James Scott. Born in Hertfordshire in 1770 and left an orphan at an early age, Scott worked diligently to become an accomplished surgeon specializing in the treatment of diseased joints and ulcerated hips. His fame spread nationwide and 'Scott's Coaches' were run from London to bring patients to him, many stopping at the Bell – a fact commemorated in this poem:

> 'So when you are ill, lacking potion or pill,
> To Bromley repair – famed spot.
> At the Bell put up pray
> Just step over the way
> And be cured by miraculous Scott.'

Opposite below: The White Hart on Charter Day, 2 September 1903. The White Hart was always at the centre of town life, and indeed the field behind the pub was the venue for many important cricket matches. County matches were played here until 1847, and Bromley Cricket Club continued playing on the ground until the end of the century. The inn was demolished in 1964 and replaced with a smaller building and shops. It finally closed in 1980 after a possible 600 years of existence.

The Royal Bell Hotel, c. 1880. This is the original Bell, demolished in 1897–8 to make way for the present hotel. It can be traced back to the seventeenth century, for it was at the Bell that the parliamentary survey of the manor was planned in 1696. The Bell is also mentioned in Jane Austen's Pride and Prejudice.

Swan and Mitre, High Street, c. 1871. This coaching inn dated from the early nineteenth century. The stables are on the left of this photograph. The inn was very popular with the carters and country carriers resting on their journey to the London markets. The seating was obtained from the Gaiety Theatre in London, and the ornate mirrors were presented by the music hall star Marie Lloyd, who was a customer.

42955. Bromley; P——— Lane. F.F.&C⁰.

Above: The Crown Inn, Plaistow. An advert in the Bromley Record for 1858 extols the virtues of the Crown's tea gardens, good stabling and dry skittle ground.

Right: The Prince Frederick, Nichol Lane, Plaistow, 10 February 1890.

Opposite above: The Tiger's Head at Mason's Hill has been dated to 1706. This building was constructed at the end of the last century. A fair was held here at Whitsun every year.

Opposite below: The Bricklayers' Arms, at the junction of Mason's Hill and Napier Road.

The Crooked Billet at Southborough, c. 1882. It is said that this building contained some brickwork dating from an earlier building, which bore the date 1617. This pub was damaged during the war and rebuilt in 1956. Both the Crooked Billet and its near neighbour the Chequers were popular with the racing fraternity, who attended meetings on Bromley Common and later at Bromley race-course at Cooper's Farm, which was established by William Pawley of the White Hart in 1864.

Opposite above: The Beech Tree, London Road, c. 1900. This pub took its name from a fine purple beech that was felled to make way for the pub.

Opposite below: Uridge's Corner, c. 1880. Uridge's grocers shop was in Widmore Road just off the Market Square. This area was widened in the scheme of 1883 at a cost of £2,500.

White Hart Corner, showing the premises of R. Skinner and E. Gould, who were homoeopathic pharmacists, 1888.

No. 11 Market Square, c. 1900. This building dates from the late eighteenth century, when it was a haberdashers. It was, for a short while, the Prince of Wales public house, and in 1880 was taken by Waterer and Dickins. The Conservative Club was housed on the first floor.

F. Hearn's butchers shop, Simpsons Road, 1923. Mr Hearn senior is in the centre while Charles Hearn, then aged 18, stands on the right. The days when meat could be hung up outside on display are long gone.

G. Pamphilon and Son, wine merchants, High Street. The building dated from the eighteenth century, but the front of the premises was rebuilt in 1876.

John King's tailors and outfitters shop at 36 High Street, 1900. Mr King is on the right, and an assistant and errand boy are in the other doorway. Mr King was known as Cheery Jack and was very popular locally. He was active in Freemasonry and was Honorary Secretary of the Bromley Bowling Club until his death in 1907.

W.T. Ashby, confectioner and tobacconist, 26 Plaistow Grove, c. 1905.

Robert L. Gore's furnishing ironmonger, Market Square, was here from 1877 to 1895. Mr Gore, seen here in the doorway, advertised in the local Strong's Directory as a bell-hanger, locksmith, gas and hot water engineer. A bell-hanger supplied and fitted the complicated system of bells used to summon servants in a large house.

A constable stops at the local coffee stall, 1900.

Bromley Co-operative Society, East Street, c. 1903.

Ferris and Sons' saddlers, 103 High Street, c. 1880. An advert in a local directory of 1885 proclaimed that 'Carriage, Gig, Tandem and every description of Harness on the Newest Principles' were available, as well as whips of every description and mourning rosettes.

Left: Edward Strong was the founder of Bromley's first newspaper, the Bromley Record and Monthly Advertiser, first published in June 1858. The first issue was of eight small pages but its initial success ensured that it grew quickly. It finally ceased publication in 1913. In 1858 Strong also published the History of Bromley, and later a series of directories from 1866 to 1905.

Below: Dunn's removal and delivery vans outside the Town Hall in Tweedy Road, c. 1929.

Harrison Gibson's furniture store in the High Street, November 1935. The store was damaged by fire in 1968 and was rebuilt.

Hadlow's Garage, at the junction of College Road and Plaistow Lane, c. 1935.

Four

Churches

St Peter and St Paul's church from the south-east, 1868. The parish church of Bromley dates back to the thirteenth century. The fourteenth-century tower of Kent flint remains, but in 1792 the rest of the church was rebuilt in red brick.

Above: In 1865 Arthur Hellicar was appointed vicar and by his efforts further changes were made to the church, culminating in the erection of a new chancel in 1883.

Left: The Bromley blitz of 16 April 1941 left eight churches in the town destroyed or severely damaged. This is St Peter and St Paul's church on the morning following the raid.

All but the fourteenth-century tower was lost. The foundation stone for a new church was laid by the Queen, then Princess Elizabeth, on 13 October 1949. The church, with the tower now at the southern end, was consecrated in December 1957.

St Mark's church, Westmoreland Road. Originally built in 1897, this was the daughter church to the parish church. It lost all but its tower in the raid of 1941. The foundation stone of the new church was laid by HRH Princess Marina on 3 June 1952.

St Luke's church, Bromley Common, c. 1925. As the population of Bromley grew rapidly during the late nineteenth century, a new town developed at Bromley Common and there was a demand for a new church. A temporary iron church was erected in 1881 on a site at the corner of Addison Road, and St Luke's grew from these humble beginnings. It was consecrated in 1890.

St John's church, Park Road, c. 1900. Built in 1880 of Kentish ragstone and brick, this replaced the first building on this site – an iron church, which had been purchased on the Isle of Wight.

Christ Church, Highland Road, c. 1890. This church, in the Early English style, was built by Mr S. Cawston of Bromley Hill, a man of strong evangelical tendencies.

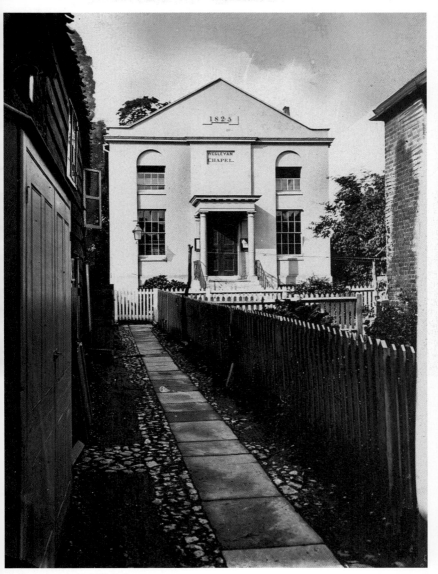

Zion chapel, 66–7 High Street.

Bromley Baptist chapel, Tweedy Road, c. 1894. The foundation stone of this chapel was laid by the famous Baptist preacher Charles Hadden Spurgeon in 1864. In 1905 school premises were built at the rear of the church at a cost of £2,000. The building on the left is the School of Science and Art, opened in 1878. The cost of this building was raised by public subscription. In 1892 the school was presented to the Local Board, and in 1894 the section of the building under the copper cupola was added as Bromley's first public library.

Opposite above: Methodist Church, High Street, c. 1881–2. Nonconformist churches sprang up in the town from the late eighteenth century. John Wesley first preached in the town in 1772 and was to visit several times. A small chapel was built at Widmore Green in 1776; then a larger site at the rear of 66–7 High Street was purchased in the 1820s, and Zion chapel, with a school-room beneath, was soon opened. In 1875 a larger Gothic-style church was built in the High Street. After a short stay in Holwood Road, Bromley Methodist church is now in College Road.

Opposite below: Congregational church, Widmore Road, c. 1900. The history of the Congregational Church in Bromley dates from 1788, when it is said that some London ministers regularly walked here to hold services. This building was the third Congregational chapel and was built in 1881 at a cost of £15,000. This church was burnt down by incendiary bombs on 16 April 1941. A new building was opened in 1948 and the present building in 1990.

St George's Church at Bickley was built in 1863. It had an imposing spire of Caen stone 175 ft high. However, this stone does not wear well and in 1905 it had to be replaced. In 1989 the church was severely damaged by fire.

Opposite above: Presbyterian church, Freelands Road. Built in 1895 with lecture halls, Sunday school classrooms and kitchens, the church has an imposing 188-ft spire.

Opposite below: St Joseph's Roman Catholic church, Plaistow Lane, opened in 1911

St George's church and vicarage from the air, c. 1930.

Central Hall, London Road. In 1881 the Farwig Wesleyan Mission was formed in a cottage at Mooreland Road. The Mission thrived and in April 1905 the Central Hall was opened at a cost of £15,000 to continue its work. The site was redeveloped in 1973.

The quadrangle, Bromley College.

Bromley College. John Warner, Bishop of Rochester and a resident of Bromley Palace, died in 1666 and left £8,500 in his will to found a college or almshouses for 'twenty poore widowes of Orthodoxe and loyalle clergymen'. The Bishop intended that the college would be in Rochester, but a suitable site could not be found so a 4-acre site near the Bishop's Palace at Bromley was chosen. There are twenty dwellings in the original building constructed around a quadrangle. For many years it was thought that this was designed by Sir Christopher Wren, but though it is known that both the master mason and the master carpenter had worked for Wren, there is no proof that he had any connection with the building. A second quadrangle of twenty houses was built in the late eighteenth century. Each of the residences consisted of two rooms, a kitchen and an attic connected by a steep spiral staircase.

Sheppard's College, c. 1900. Many of the widows here lived with spinster daughters as companions. In 1841 Sophia Sheppard, realizing the plight of the daughters on the death of their mothers, built a terrace of five houses for them. In 1971 the charter was amended so that Bromley College could accept retired clergymen and their wives, and after a scheme of modernization the Queen Mother visited the college in 1977 to inspect the new homes.

Five

Farming

Springhill Farm, College Road, c. 1883. The house and estate of Springhill can be dated back to the seventeenth century. This carefully posed photograph by S.P. Webber, the founder of Bromley Camera Club, demonstrates that even by the late nineteenth century Bromley was still a rural area.

Opposite above: Bromley Palace oasthouses. Mr Coles Child bought Bromley Palace and the estates from the Ecclesiastical Commissioners in 1845. He modernized the farm and took great pride in being the first to supply the London market with hops each year. The hop fields themselves were midway between the town and Bickley, while the oasthouses and farmhouse were situated to the south of Widmore Lane. The oasthouses were demolished in 1927.

Opposite below: Crosswood Freeholders, 30 April 1922. Allotments became very popular between the wars, and often allotment holders organized themselves into local groups.

"Crosswood" FREEHOLDERS.
APRIL 30TH - 1922.

Haymaking near Bourne Vale, Hayes.

Opposite above: Bencewell Farm, Oakley Road, Bromley Common.

Opposite below: Tan-stripping in Oakley Woods, Bromley Common, c. 1886. Tannin was used in the preparation of leather and in some inks. It was obtained from oak galls and the bark of some trees.

Bencewell Farm, Bromley Common.

Frank Price was a shepherd to the Hambro family of Hayes Place for thirty-eight years. In the 1920s he lost a hand in a threshing machine accident. Price used to lead the Hayes May Queen

Six

Local Services

National Schools, Bromley, c. 1869. This building, opened in 1855 at a cost of £2,700, replaced the school built in 1814. It was intended to accommodate 450 children but was very soon full, and was enlarged in 1871. This view was taken from Stiddolph's Nursery Gardens.

Bickley and Widmore Infants School, Tylney Road, c. 1905.

Bromley Church of England School, c. 1933

Left: Holy Trinity Convent School, Plaistow Lane, c. 1922.

Below: Bromley County Girls School, c. 1908. This school was founded in 1905 under the headmistress Miss Walters, seen here with her prefects.

Bromley County Girls School, art class, c. 1922.

Playing fields at Bromley County Girls School, Nightingale Lane, Bickley, c. 1922.

Old Town Hall, 7 July 1929. In 1863 the Lord of the Manor, Mr Coles Child, indicated a desire that there should be an imposing town hall for Bromley. The cost of the building was £10,000 and the foundation stone was laid by Mr Child's infant son on 7 November 1863. The basement formed part of the market, while on the south side was the police station. On the ground floor were offices, and on the first floor was the hall itself, 60 ft long by 30 ft wide.

Opposite: The town pump, 1 July 1929. This Victorian iron water pump was installed next to the Town Hall, replacing the one that had stood in the centre of the market-place until 1863. This pump was removed to the Church House Gardens in 1933, where it remained until its return to the market-place in 1985.

Far left: Henry Checkley, Town Crier, c. 1890. By profession Checkley was a boot and shoe mender who hired out a pony chaise and bath chair. He was the local bill-sticker and Bromley's last town crier.

Left: Checkley was also Bromley's last beadle, and on Sunday mornings stood at the parish church lych-gate wearing a long braided frock coat with gilt buttons, white choker and gold braided hat, carrying his tall staff of office surmounted by a golden crown. Checkley died about 1896 and is buried at Reading.

The Bromley Local Board was first elected in 1867. A plot of land was obtained between East and West Street and this building was erected as its headquarters.

Opening of the new Town Hall, 25 September 1907. This was built in the 'Free Georgian style' on the site of Widmore House, the home of Colonel J. Newman Tweedy. The municipal portion was on Tweedy Road and the courts were at the rear. The total cost, including the furnishings, was £35,000. The building was formally opened by the Mayor, Alderman R.W. James JP.

Bromley Borough Council, c. 1918.

Council Chamber, 1918–19. A spacious room, panelled in Italian walnut and containing stained glass that incorporated the Borough Arms, it was positioned in the building to be far away from the noise of the street.

Above: Beating the bounds in Bromley can be traced back to 1772, when an entry in the Parish Vestry Book records that this custom was carried out in April of that year. Although it became a ceremonial occasion there was a purpose behind the custom, as it impressed on everyone, particularly the children, the parish boundaries. The beating of the boundary posts and marks was carried out by children armed with white sticks, and some were bumped on the posts by the assembled company. The day normally ended with dinner in the Bell Inn. The last recorded performance of this custom was in 1890.

Below: Bromley Gas Works, Homesdale Road. The foundation stone of the new retort house was laid in 1879. Robinson Latter, clerk to the Local Board, is holding the brick.

Central Library, High Street, c. 1908. The first Bromley public library was established in an annexe of the School of Science and Art building in Tweedy Road in 1894 (see p. 79). In 1903 the philanthropist Andrew Carnegie offered the sum of £7,500 for the purpose of erecting a new public library. Mrs Emily Dowling (1819–1900) had left her house, Neelgherries, to the inhabitants of Bromley in her will, and this site on the High Street was thought suitable for the new library. It was opened by Andrew Carnegie on 29 May 1906. As E.L.S. Horsburgh wrote in his history of Bromley, 'the erection of this building [is] one of the most notable landmarks in the history of the town.'

Central Library, High Street, c. 1967. This was demolished in 1969 to make way for the new Central Library, opened on 13 April 1977. The site is shared by the Churchill Theatre, which was opened by Prince Charles on 19 July 1977.

Right: The post office in East Street was first occupied by the ever expanding post office staff in 1897. By 1909 there were twenty-four indoor staff, eighty-five outdoor and fifteen telegraph boys to be accommodated.

Below: Staff at Hayes post office, c. 1910. Robert Pearce, the postmaster, middle row on the left, is seen here with his two daughters, Bessie and Amy, and staff. He joined the Postal Service in 1894, and when he retired in 1934 he must have been one of the oldest postmen in England.

Bromley Fire Brigade, 1897. A meeting was held in the Town Hall in 1866 with the intention of forming a volunteer fire brigade. The personnel were largely drawn from the 18th Kent Rifle Volunteers and they had their headquarters at the White Hart. A steam-powered pumping engine was purchased in 1897, when the brigade was taken over by the Urban District Council. In 1904 the Volunteer Fire Brigade was replaced by a permanent body of fire-fighters.

Fire station and Municipal Buildings, c. 1923. In 1910 the fire station and stables in West Street were replaced by this building at a cost of £5,191 12s. 8d.

Fire station, South Street. This building is still in use today.

Bromley Special Constables, c. 1918. Complete with cat, this photograph was taken at the side of the police station.

Street cleaner at Henry Street, c. 1900.

Bromley Cottage Hospital. In 1869 a committee was established to found a hospital for the district. Initially two cottages were purchased in Pieter's Lane, now renamed Cromwell Avenue. In 1875 a larger hospital was needed, and so the cottages were demolished and this building erected.

The Queen's Gardens and Homoeopathic Hospital. The hospital was opened on a site opposite the Town Hall in 1889 as a memorial to Dr Robert Phillips, who operated a homoeopathic dispensary in the town. The original building was damp and unsuitable, and in 1900 this building was erected on part of the White Hart Field, which Mr Coles Child had presented to the town. The Phillips Memorial Hospital was demolished in 1959.

Bromley War Memorial, on Martin's Hill, was dedicated by General Lord Horne and the Lord Bishop of Rochester on Sunday 29 October 1922. The names of 857 men from Bromley who died in the First World War were inscribed on the memorial.

Opposite above: Victory Celebrations outside the Railway Signal, Mason's Hill, Monday 11 November 1918.

Opposite below: Peace Celebrations, High Street, c. 1919. The parade passes the Royal Bell Hote

The Home Guard, No. 3 Platoon (Keston), C Company, 52nd Kent Battalion, The Queens Own Royal West Kent Regiment. After the group photograph they were off to the Fox for a pint.

Opposite above: Inspection of the Civil Defence Volunteers by the Duke of Kent, 27 May 1941

Opposite below: ARP Post A.18 was sited at Bromley Library. H. Alderton, the borough librarian, is seated in the centre.

Coney Hall Auxiliary Fire Service. The AFS was initiated to support the regular fire service. They supplied local cover while the regulars fought fires in London during the Blitz. The pumps were often pulled by commandeered builders' lorries.

Coney Hall Auxiliary Fire Service. At the height of the Blitz members of the AFS were sent to London. On 13 March 1941 five members from Coney Hall were killed in east London. They were buried together at West Wickham.

Seven

Railways

Bromley South station, c. 1870. The railway age arrived in Bromley on 3 May 1858, when a large crowd assembled on Martin's Hill to watch the first train leave Shortlands station on the West End and Crystal Palace Railway. The same year the Mid-Kent Railway Company opened a route to St Mary Cray via Bromley, and this station at the southern end of the town was built.

Bromley South station. In 1861 the London, Chatham and Dover Company secured a monopoly over the line to St Mary Cray. In 1894 the new station building at Bromley South was erected.

Bromley South station footbridge, c. 1862.

Sundridge Park station, Plaistow Lane, was opened on 1 January 1878, but was called Plaistow until 1894.

Bromley North station, c. 1925. On the branch line to Grove Park, this station opened on 1 January 1878. The station was rebuilt in 1925 by the Southern Railway Company just before electrification of the line.

Hayes station, here seen under construction, was opened in May 1882.

Eight

Leisure

RECREATION GROUND, BROMLEY.

Martin's Hill Recreation Ground. Martin's Hill, sloping down to the River Ravensbourne, was owned by the Ecclesiastical Commissioners. In 1878 there was a rumour in the town that the site was to be redeveloped. The townspeople objected, writing articles and poems:

> 'On this, the people's piece of land,
> May builder never ply his skill,
> May never innovating hand
> Deprive the town of Martin's Hill.'

The Local Board made representation to the Commissioners and secured the site for £2,500.

Martin's Hill entrance to the Recreation Ground, c. 1920. The war memorial was not erected until 1922.

Martin's Hill, c. 1910. In 1887, to celebrate Queen Victoria's Jubilee, the Hop Garden and meadow below Martin's Hill were purchased for £4,600 and renamed Queen's Mead. In the distance could be seen the Crystal Palace.

"Neelgherries" Bromley.

Library Gardens, High Street, c. 1918. The grounds around the new library, opened in 1906 on the site of Neelgherries, were laid out as a public park. The rear of the library can be seen in the picture.

The bandstand, Library Gardens.

Children's boating pool, Church House Gardens. The Library Gardens and the grounds of Church House, destroyed in 1941, were amalgamated to form the present gardens.

Lyric Theatre, High Street, opened on 4 February 1889. It was originally known as the Grand Hall and could seat 900 people. It was to undergo many name changes, to the Lyric Theatre in 1905, to the Grand again in 1926, and finally to the New Theatre in 1947. Many famous actors and music hall stars have appeared here including Albert Chevalier, Bryan Forbes, Cliff Richard, George Cole, Denholm Elliott, Sheila Hancock and the Twerps Concert Party!

New Theatre, c. 1967. During the Second World War the theatre was used as an air raid shelter. People would congregate in the old swimming pool, which was under the theatre itself.

Opposite above: The New Theatre was destroyed by fire in May 1971. Bromley was to be without a theatre until the Churchill Theatre was opened in 1977.

Opposite below: The Drill Hall, East Street, was opened in 1872 as the drill hall for the 18th Kent Rifle Corps. The opening of the hall was celebrated by a grand concert at which Mr Arthur Sullivan, then aged 30, was the accompanist.

The Gaumont, High Street, 1961. This cinema was opened on Monday 23 November 1936. Complete with a 150-seat café restaurant, a mighty Compton organ, a kiddies' club and the latest film technology, the Gaumont was assured of success. It finally closed in 1961.

Opposite above: Hervey Lodge 1692, c. 1885. This Masonic Lodge was founded in 1877.

Opposite below: Bromley Girl Guides, c. 1919.

Peter Nesbit was a carrier between Bromley and Beckenham. To celebrate the wedding of the Prince of Wales to Princess Alexandra in March 1863 he ate a giant pie outside the White Hart. The pie consisted of 5 lb of rumpsteak, 4 lb of flour, 11 lb of lard and four large potatoes. He washed all this down with half a gallon of ale. He survived until 1867!

Opposite above: A fête at South Hill Wood, Shortlands, c. 1904.

Opposite below: Queen's Mead at the foot of Martin's Hill, c. 1900. This was a popular venue for fêtes and other events.

Above: Sundridge Park Social Club, Burnt Ash Lane.

Below: Sanger's Circus arrives in Bromley, September 1898.

The Bromley Cricket Club played for many years on the cricket ground behind the White Hart. By the late nineteenth century this field was not big enough to accommodate all who wanted to play. The Cricket Club moved to a new ground at Plaistow Lane, and this photograph was taken in 1902 soon after the completion of the pavilion.

Bromley Bowling Club, c. 1920. This club was formed at a meeting at the Bell Hotel on 18 April 1889.

Cycle Championship, c. 1895. This was held at the Cricket Club ground at Widmore Road.

Bromley Cycle Club sports, Widmore, c. 1897.

Keston Ponds Swimming Club, c. 1913. This club met regularly at the ponds between 1910 and 1919. They constructed diving stages on either side of the middle pond.

Bromley Open Air Swimming Pool, Southborough Road. It took thirty years to build a municipal swimming pool in Bromley, and it was opened in 1925. It was 150 ft long by 60 ft wide. The cost was £8,680.

Nine

Hayes

Hayes Place, west front, c. 1920. The original Hayes Place was built in 1624 on a site opposite the parish church. William Pitt bought the house and began to rebuild it in 1756, the year before he became prime minister. His son, William Pitt the younger, was born here on 28 May 1759 and was baptized in the parish church. The family moved to Somerset in 1766 but the house was later bought again by Pitt the elder, by then the Earl of Chatham, and he died there in May 1778.

The library, Hayes Place, c. 1920. The last occupant was Sir E.A. Hambro. On his death in 1925 the parkland was sold for development, and the house itself was demolished in 1933.

Hayes Court, c. 1935. Built in West Common Road in 1776, Hayes Court was the seat of Sir Vicary Gibbs from 1751 to 1820. In the 1920s it was a girls school, and from 1946 it has been a trade union headquarters.

St Mary the Virgin, Hayes, dates from around 1200. The fourteenth-century spire was blown down in the early eighteenth century, and the present spire of oak shingles was erected in 1861. At a similar date the exterior was encased in flint as part of a restoration by Sir George Gilbert Scott.

The Rectory, Hayes, was built in the eighteenth century. It was first used as the public library for the Hayes area in 1946.

Post office, Baston Road, looking north. The post office opened in 1883.

Baston Road, looking south, c. 1930. St Mary's Cottages are in the distance, with the post office on the right.

Hayes Street, looking north, before 1936.

Hayes Street, looking north, before 1936.

Hayes Street, c. 1950.

The Walnut Tree. This eighteenth-century cottage has been used as a shop for many years, first a bakery and corn chandlers and then a newsagent and sweet shop.

Station Approach, c. 1950. The original Hayes station was opened on Whit Monday 1882. The Ordnance Survey map of 1933 shows that the only buildings in this area were the station and the New Inn. The later edition of 1936 shows Station Approach flanked by shops and the new picture house.

May Queen processions through Hayes, c. 1934. This annual event, held on the second Saturday in May, was devised in 1913 by Mr Deedy, a folklore enthusiast. Many areas elected their own May Queen and sent them to Hayes, where the May Queen of London was crowned.

New Inn, c. 1905. On the site of an old beerhouse, this pub attracted customers from the railway station opposite.

Opposite above: New Inn, after 1936. In 1935 the old pub was demolished and this 'baronial style' roadhouse was built. Badly damaged by enemy action in 1940, it was reopened in 1962. It was subsequently remodelled in the 1980s.

Opposite below: The George Inn. It is thought that there was an alehouse here in 1671, and it is possible to trace the name 'George' back to 1759. A local legend states that at one time the inn sign was painted by J.E. Millais, who was to become a famous member of the Royal Academy. The inn was popular with carriers and coachmen, and on Whit Tuesday a fair was held outside.

THE NEW INN
HAYES. 6½

ENRIGH SERIES

Hayes

The George Inn, c. 1950. The freehold of the inn was purchased by Watneys from the Hambro family in 1927. Today it is a restaurant.

Hayes Hill Estate was developed during the 1930s, and was popular with those seeking a country lifestyle away from the city.

Ten

Keston

The Fox, Keston Common, c. 1908. Keston Common was very popular with day trippers, and many people would come to spend the day walking here and taking tea in the local cafés and tearooms. For those who preferred something stronger, the Fox, rebuilt in 1889, was an attraction.

The Greyhound, Keston Common, c. 1912. This public house developed in the latter part of the century from a beerhouse. It was demolished in 1938.

Keston Common was an agricultural community, and at certain times of the year the farmer and his men would go 'yowling'. They would encircle a tree and drink the following toast:

> 'Here's to thee old apple-tree!
> Hence thou mayst bud and where thou mayst blow;
> And whence thou mayst bear apples enow!
> Hats full! Caps full!
> Bushel, bushel, stocks full!
> And by pockets full too! Hurrah!'

Commonside. On the left can be seen St Audrey's church, built by Lord Sackville Cecil in 1888 as a private church. Lord Sackville lived in Hayes and it is said he argued with the rector, resolving never to set foot in his church again. Therefore he built this church just inside the Keston parish boundary. He also converted some adjacent buildings into a parish reading room and gymnasium. The church is now a private home.

Heathfield Road. The Fox is on the right, and one of the many tea rooms in the area is on the left.

Keston church. In 1950 repair work to war damage at the church revealed four shallow pre-Norman graves. These suggest that this was an important burial site, and that the church is at least Norman in origin. The church dedication is not known and was lost before the parish registers began in 1540. The church has seven bells in the small tower. Also damaged during the war were three of the four windows by William Morris and Co.; only 'Love' by Burne Jones survives.

Keston windmill. This, the last of three windmills that originally stood in the Keston parish, is one of the few old Kentish post-mills now remaining. It was built in 1716 and, being in a corn producing area, worked steadily until the sweeps were damaged in a gale in 1878.

Keston windmill and Heathfield Road, c. 1903.

Wilberforce Oak. The first large estate in the parish was Holwood. From 1785 to 1801 this was the home of William Pitt the younger, who had been born in Hayes. In the grounds of his house was this oak tree, where it was reputed that Pitt's friend William Wilberforce resolved to work to abolish the slave trade. The seat, erected in 1862, bears his words.

The central figure in this group of people visiting the Wilberforce Oak is the first black bishop to be appointed, Samuel Crowther. Crowther was consecrated Bishop of the Niger Territory in 1864. He died in Lagos in 1891.

Keston Ponds and Caesar's Well. It is said that when Caesar's army was encamped on Holwood Hill it was in need of water. A soldier saw a raven alight near the camp and search the turf; he presumed that the bird was looking for water and subsequently discovered the stream – hence its name the Ravensbourne. The ponds were made at the beginning of the nineteenth century by Mr John Ward, the owner of Holwood, to supply his house with water.

Keston Ponds, c. 1950. Lord Stanley presented the ponds and an area of common to the parish in 1926.

Acknowledgements

All the photographs in this book have been taken from the Illustrations Collection of Bromley Local Studies. Thanks are due to those people who have donated or lent photographs to this magnificent collection.

I an indebted to the work of E.L.S. Horsburgh and more recently Patricia Knowlden for source material for the captions, to the staff of Local Studies for their patient assistance during the preparation of this book and, finally, to my daughter Laura, who likes writing books as much as I do.